Is Enochian Magick Right for You?

The ultimate goal of the Enochian Magician is to become a living embodiment of spiritual knowledge and power. Enochian Magick works by employing techniques which strengthen the will and give control over the mind, allowing a magician to bring about personal changes as well as changes for others.

By learning techniques to travel the astral plane in your "Body of Light," you will encounter the principles that create and sustain existence: the Angelic rulers who inhabit the four Watchtowers and thirty Aethyrs of the subtle regions of the universe. From these powerful beings, you can learn to manifest your purpose in life and to tread the path from the physical world of mortality to the spiritual world of immortality.

There are no requirements to Enochian Magick but one: that you channel your spiritual energy to look deep within yourself. It is a system for undertaking the great work of recognizing and conversing with your inner divinity, also known as your Holy Guardian Angel. When you understand your true nature and capacity as a spiritual being through knowledge of your own divinity, all things are possible.

GW00686369

About the Authors

Together Gerald and Betty Schueler have together written many articles and books on enochian magic subject matter. Gerald has been a member of the Theosophical Society for over twenty-five years studying both Egyptian Magick and hieroglyphics. The Schuelers currently reside in Maryland.

To Write to the Authors

If you wish to contact the authors or would like more information about this book, please write to the author in care of Llewellyn Worldwide, and we will forward your request. Both the author and publisher appreciate hearing from you and learning of your enjoyment of this book and how it has helped you. Llewellyn Worldwide cannot guarantee that every letter written to the author can be answered, but all will be forwarded. Please write to:

Gerald & Betty Schueler
% Llewellyn Worldwide
P.O. Box 64383 L716, St. Paul, MN 55164-0383, U.S.A.

Please enclose a self-addressed, stamped envelope for reply,
or $1.00 to cover costs.
If outside the U.S.A., enclose international postal reply coupon.

Free Catalog from Llewellyn

For more than 90 years, Llewellyn has brought its readers knowledge in the fields of metaphysics and human potential. Learn about the newest books in spiritual guidance, natural healing, astrology, occult philosophy and more. Enjoy book reviews, new age articles, a calendar of events, plus current advertised products and services. To get your free copy of Llewellyn's New Worlds of Mind and Spirit, send your name and address to:

Llewellyn's New Worlds of Mind and Spirit
P.O. Box 64383 L716, St. Paul, MN 55164-0383, U.S.A.

The Truth About

Enochian Magick

by Gerald & Betty Schueler

1996
Llewellyn Publications
St. Paul, MN 55164-0383, U.S.A.

The Truth About Enochian Magick © 1993 by Llewellyn Publications. All rights reserved. No part of this book may be reproduced or used in any manner whatsoever without written permission from Llewellyn Publications, except in the case of brief quotations embodied in critical articles and reviews.

For permissions, serialization, condensation or adaptations, write to the publisher.

FIRST EDITION, 1993
SECOND EDITION
First Printing, 1996

Cover design by Maria Mazzara

International Standard Book Number:
0-87542-716-2

LLEWELLYN PUBLICATIONS
A Division of Llewellyn Worldwide, Ltd.
P.O. Box 64383, St. Paul, MN 55164-0383

Other books by Gerald and Betty Schueler

INTRODUCTION TO
ENOCHIAN MAGICK

Magick is broadly defined as the science and art of causing change to occur in conformity with the will. Any time we will something to happen, and that something comes about, we have conducted a magical operation. In truth, therefore, we are all magicians. We conduct magical operations all day long, and take them for granted.

The reason we take most of our willed actions for granted is that we are well aware of the means by which the action comes about. For example, suppose you are thirsty, and you will want a drink of water. By filling a glass with water and drinking it, you have brought about a willed change. Although this is an overly simplistic example, it demonstrates the fundamental principle of Magick—the directed will can bring about a change through any suitable means.

Magick asserts that there is no such thing as a miracle. The "suitable means" through which magical operations work are always in accordance with natural law. When well-known laws or principles are used, we tend to denigrate the action as mundane. Conversely, when little-known laws or principles are used, we tend to elevate the action from anywhere between the

1

magical and the miraculous. In reality, all of the laws of the universe are equal; it is only our ignorance of those lesser-known laws that makes their successful use so spectacular.

There are many schools of Magick, each teaching from a different angle and emphasizing different aspects of western occultism, whose fountain source lies in ancient Egypt. One branch, or school, is the Enochian. As you would expect, Enochian Magick shares a great deal of its teachings with other schools, especially the Qabalistic. Its central message is similar to that of most major religions: there exists a path which leads us from the physical world of mortality upward into the spiritual world of immortality. The fundamental teachings of Enochian Magick address ways in which to tread this path.

WHAT IS THE PURPOSE OF ENOCHIAN MAGICK?

The only legitimate purpose in the practice of Enochian Magick, as with any school of Magick, is the spiritualization of consciousness. It is the Great Work of recognizing our inner divinity and then conversing with it. This inner spark of divinity is known as our *holy guardian angel*. A major stage of the Work is called *knowledge* and *conversation with one's holy guardian angel*. Every ritual and exercise used by the sincere magician should be a step along the royal road of the Great Work.

WHO SHOULD USE ENOCHIAN MAGICK?

Enochian Magick is but one of many paths to spiritual enlightenment. Because each path is different and has its own unique problems of ascension, each individual must seek the most appropriate path for him or herself. This can only be done by taking logical, dispassionate consideration of the paths available.

Some paths offer spiritual rewards in return for a life of self-denial. Others offer rewards for those who dedicate their lives to serving humankind. Others, like Enochian Magick, require that the individual look deep inside and come to understand his or her true nature. There are no other requirements. What that individual does with their life, once they understand their true nature, is up to the individual. Some will choose to pursue the spiritual world; others will use their new understanding to help humankind. There is no right or wrong choice. Everyone can help further the spiritual advancement of humankind in his or her own way.

A BRIEF HISTORY OF
ENOCHIAN MAGICK

Enochian Magick was first presented to the public in modern times by Sir John Dee, the court astrologer to Queen Elizabeth of England. Dee was born in England in 1527, and was a magician as well as an astrologer. Working with Edward Kelly (sometimes spelled Kelley), his psychic associate and partner, Dee "discovered" the system of Enochian Magick. According to Dee's diary, the magical system was revealed to him by the Enochian Angels that inhabited the Watchtowers and Aethyrs of the subtle regions of the universe.

While Kelly conducted the psychic operations known as skrying, Dee kept meticulous records of everything that occurred. Kelly would look deeply into a crystal "shewstone" and describe aloud whatever he saw. Dee, in turn, carefully wrote everything down. The shewstone of Dee and Kelly is believed to have been a black crystal about the size of an egg. Although objects such as water and mirrors can often be used to skry successfully, the favored material is crystal. Dee is credited with having been one of the first magicians to use a large polished spherical crystal—a crystal ball.

The net result of Dee's research was a series of tablets sectioned into squares with runes on each square. These runes were the letters of the Enochian alphabet. They spelled out the names of the deities who presided over the regions symbolized by the squares. The tablets were thus devised as maps of the invisible spheres that surround our physical world (see Figure 1).

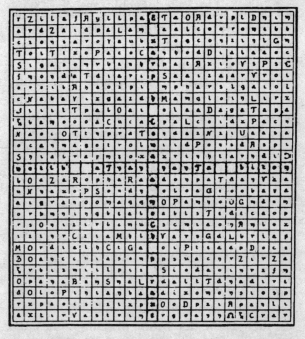

Figure 1. Four Great Watchtowers connected by the Black Cross

Little became of Dee's work until late in the nineteenth century, when it was incorporated and adopted by a mysterious and highly secret brother-hood of adepts in England, who called themselves the Hermetic Order of the Golden Dawn. They invoked the Enochian deities whose names were written on the tablets. They also traveled in what they called their Body of Light (a poetic term for the aura) into these subtle regions and recorded their psychic experiences in a scientific manner. One member, who left the Order to found his own, traveled through each of the thirty Aethyrs. His name was Aleister Crowley, and he carefully recorded his travels through the Aethyrs in a book called *The Vision and the Voice*. This book was written with highly symbolic imagery, and most people find it too difficult to understand or put to practical use.

The book, *Enochian Magick: A Practical Manual* (Schueler, Llewellyn Publications), was written in an effort to eliminate the unnecessary complexity of the Enochian magickal system and to combine its numerous elements into a single source. This book, published as a part of Llewellyn's High Magick series, contains fundamental teachings of Enochian Magick such as the derivation of deity names, the rules associated with deriving signposts (known characteristics of the Watchtowers and

Aethyrs of Enochian Magick), and step-by-step techniques for invocations. This book was followed by *An Advanced Guide to Enochian Magick*, which includes the main rituals and formulae of Enochian Magick. A third book, *Enochian Physics*, describes the structure of the Enochian magickal universe and compares that with the latest theories of modern physics. A fourth book, *Enochian Tarot*, was published in 1989.

THE ENOCHIAN ALPHABET

The Enochian (or Angelic) alphabet contains twenty-one magical letters. It is unrelated to any previous lettering system such as Latin, Greek, Hebrew, or any of the established magical alphabets. To some, it appears to be a series of Qabalistic pictographs meant to be imagined visually, and not commonly inscribed. The Enochian language has a unique grammar and syntax structure. Each letter has correspondences as shown in the following table.

The creators of this language are unknown to us, lost in the mists of time. Some people believe that it originated on the lost continent of Atlantis. Whatever the origin, its letters constitute the Language of the Angels. The rules of pronunciation are:

1. Most consonants are followed by "eh" (B is "beh," D is "deh").

2. Most vowels are followed by "h" (A is "ah," O is "oh").

3. In general, each letter forms a syllable.

The letters *Y* and *I* are interchangeable with each other, as are *V* with *U* and *S* with *Z*. (*which* is pronounced "zod.") *S* is pronounced either "ess" or "seh." *R* can be either "reh," "rah," or "ar." *I* is pronounced "ee" (*TI* is "teh-ee" or simply "tee").

Enochian Alphabet Correspondences

Letter	Zodiac/Element	Tarot
A	Taurus	Hierophant
B	Aries	Star
C,K	Fire	Judgement
D	Spirit	Empress
E	Virgo	Hermit
F	Cauda Draconis	Juggler
G	Cancer	Chariot
H	Air	Fool
I,J,Y	Sagittarius	Temperance
L	Cancer	Chariot
M	Aquarius	Emperor
N	Scorpio	Death
O	Libra	Justice
P	Leo	Strength
Q	Water	Hanged Man
R	Pisces	Moon
S	Gemini	Lovers

Letter	Zodiac/Element	Tarot
T	Leo	Strength
T	Caput Draconis	High Priestess
U,V,W	Capricorn	Devil
X	Earth	Universe
Z	Leo	Strength
	Caput Draconis	High Priestess

WHAT ARE THE WATCHTOWERS AND AETHYRS?

Enochian Magick teaches that divinity expresses itself downward from the spiritual world into the material world of time, space and form. This descent results in a graduated series of planes and subplanes until the lowest expression is reached—the physical world in which we live. These planes are called the Cosmic Planes of Manifestation. They are invisible to the five physical senses of sight, sound, smell, taste and touch, but are real nonetheless. They consist of five main planes. These cosmic planes contain the Four Great Watchtowers of Enochian Magick. A Tablet of Union unites the four Watchtowers (see Figure 1) and each of the four Watchtower Tablets. The Tablet of Union contain Squares. Each Watchtower Tablet consists of thirteen rows and twelve columns, making a total of 156 Squares. Each Square is a subplane of the Magickal Universe and holds one or more letters of the Angelic alphabet. By appropriate application of these letters, the names of all of the Enochian deities (as well as all the terrible demons) are made known.

THE WATCHTOWER OF EARTH

The Great Northern Quadrant of Earth is the first of the mighty Watchtowers that create and sustain our physical world. The Watchtower of Earth is a region of powerful formative forces that gives rise to all material things, and yet is not those things itself. The Watchtower of Earth is not the planet on which we live in our bodies of flesh. It is invisible to our eyes. Our ears hear none of its music. Our noses cannot smell its fragrances. But the subtle body, called the Body of Light, *can* see its splendors, hear its sounds and smell its odors. The Watchtower of Earth is located on the etheric plane and has astrological relationships with the Moon.

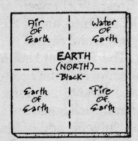 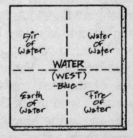

Figure 2. Watchtower of Earth   **Figure 3. Watchtower of Water**

THE WATCHTOWER OF WATER

The Great Western Quadrant of Water is the Watchtower that reflects images into our physical world—a region of strong creative life forces that gives rise to all living things—but not life itself. It is not the water we drink in the physical world. It is invisible. The Watchtower of Water is located on the astral plane and has astrological relationships with the planet Venus.

THE WATCHTOWER OF AIR

The Great Eastern Quadrant of Air is the Watchtower that pours thoughts and ideas into our physical world. It is the region of intelligent forces that gives rise to the logic and reason of all living things. The Watchtower of Air is not the air that we breathe in the physical world. It is invisible to our eyes. The Watchtower of Air is located on the lower mental plane and has astrological relationships with the planet Mercury.

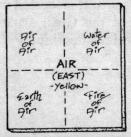

Figure 4. Watchtower of Air

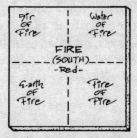

Figure 5. Watchtower of Fire

THE WATCHTOWER OF FIRE

The Great Southern Quadrant of Fire is the Watchtower that causes the constant change of our physical world. It is a region of strong creative and destructive forces that gives rise to the ultimate growth of all living things. The Watchtower of Fire is not the fire we kindle in the physical world. It is invisible to our eyes. The Watchtower of Fire is located on the upper mental plane (sometimes called the causal plane), which is just below the Great Outer Abyss. It is said to have astrological relationships with the Sun.

THE TABLET OF UNION

The Tablet of Union is the Great Tablet that is the ultimate source of all things that exist in our physical world. It is a region of strong causative forces that gives rise to the entire universe of living things. The Tablet of Union is composed entirely of spirit. It is located in the spiritual plane above the Great Outer Abyss, and has astrological relationships with our Milky Way galaxy.

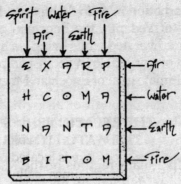

Figure 6. Tablet of Union

THE Thirty AETHYRS

Interpenetrating these Watchtowers (but separate from them) are thirty special zones called the *Aethyrs*, or *Aires*. These range from TEX, the lowest, which interfaces our Earth, to the highest, LIL, which interfaces the world of divinity. The Enochian magician learns to leave his or her physical body and travel through these Aethyrs in his or her Body of Light—the aura of modern occultism and Theosophy. As this happens, the principles that create and sustain existence manifest themselves to the traveler. He or she learns what life is all about, and what his or her purpose in life is to be. He or she can then learn the lessons of manifested existence and free him or herself from the forces of karma and reincarnation in a single lifetime. Like the *jiva-mukti* of Vedanta, the Enochian magician can become liberated while living—a living embodiment of spiritual knowledge and power. This is the ultimate goal of Enochian Magick.

THE RELATIONSHIPS OF THE WATCHTOWERS

The five main regions of the Magickal Universe, as defined in Enochian Magick, are shown in the table below.

The Cosmic Planes of Enochian Magick

Enochian	Occult
Earth	physical plane
Watchtower of Earth	etheric plane
Watchtower of Water	astral plane
Watchtower of Air	mental plane
Watchtower of Fire	causal plane
Tablet of Union	spiritual plane

Some of the major correspondences with the four Watchtowers are as follows:

Watchtower Correspondences

Watchtower	Earth	Water	Air	Fire
Plane	Physical	Astral	Mental	Spiritual
Property	Cold	Cold	Hot	Hot
	Dry	Wet	Wet	Dry
Quadrant	Northern	Western	Eastern	Southern
Color	Black	Blue	Yellow	Red

THE FOUR MAGICK WEAPONS

The practice of Enochian Magick requires the use of a Wand. However, it is preferable to use all four main magickal weapons (one for each of the four Watchtowers). You should make your own weapons, or at least inscribe appropriate sigils and/or designs on them yourself.

1. The Wand (Figure 7) represents the will of the magician. In Enochian Magick, the Wand is the weapon of Fire and is used for operations in the Watchtower of Fire.

2. The Sword (Figure 8) represents the magician's mind. In Enochian Magick, the Sword is the weapon of Air and is used for operations in the Watchtower of Air. (The Sword is sometimes replaced with the Dagger, its alternate.)

3. The Cup (Figure 9) represents the understanding and compassion of the magician. In Enochian Magick, the Cup is the weapon of Water and is used for operations in the Watchtower of Water.

4. The Pantacle (Figure 10) represents the magician's body. In Enochian Magick, the Pantacle is the weapon of Earth and is used for operations in the Watchtower of Earth.

The four main magick weapons are pictured on the following page.

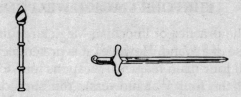

Figure 7. The Wand   **Figure 8. The Sword**

Figure 10. The Pantacle   **Figure 9. The Cup**

Correspondences of the Weapons

Weapon	Magician	Element
Wand	Spirit	Fire
Sword	Mind	Air
Cup	Emotions	Water
Pantacle	Body	Earth

THE THREE FUNDAMENTAL LAWS OF ENOCHIAN MAGIC

The three fundamental Laws of Enochian Magick are stated in H. P. Blavatsky's *The Secret Doctrine.* These Laws pertain to everything in the universe, from subatomic particles to galaxies:

1. The Law of Duality states that an omnipresent, eternal, boundless and immutable Principle splits into two aspects of itself as an act of creation in order to form the manifested worlds. This First Principle, or Infinite and Eternal Cause, splits into the duality of space and motion. All manifestation is therefore dualistic.

2. The Law of Periodicity states that the universe is a boundless plane of periodic manifestation. Everything in the universe is subject to periodic flux and reflux, ebb and flow, day and night, life and death, and so on. This continuous oscillation is an expression of the Great Breath.

3. The Law of Identity states that there is a fundamental unity among all manifested things; the differences that we observe in the universe are due solely to time and space. This Law is borne of the fact that if we choose any two objects and negate those differences due to time and space, the two objects will be

observed as one single object. The primary conclusion from this Law is that humankind is inherently a star. An important corollary of this Law is the Law of Karma—the Cycle of Necessity that defines the specific nature of each object's evolutionary progress.

THE ENOCHIAN MONAD MODEL

The model of the universe used to explain Enochian Magick is called the Enochian Monad Model. The Monad is a single, indivisible consciousness center above the first and highest Aethyr. When this Monad descends into the Aethyrs, it divides itself into two dualistic parts: a subjective consciousness center, or Self, and its objective environment, or World. The model produces the following ten axioms:

1. First Enochian Axiom: Humankind and every entity in existence, is in essence a Monad. This monadic essence expresses itself as a subjective Self and as an objective World.

2. Second Enochian Axiom: Humankind's geometric equivalent is the sphere. The center of the sphere is the Self. The surface of the sphere is the World.

3. Third Enochian Axiom: The Self is conscious individuality.

4. Fourth Enochian Axiom: The World is where the Self finds itself at any given point in time and space.

5. Fifth Enochian Axiom: Every geometric point in space is a Monad at some stage of self-expression.

6. Sixth Enochian Axiom: Any Self can communicate with any other Self, insofar as their Worlds intersect.

7. Seventh Enochian Axiom: A World is defined as a set of intersections of a host of Worlds at any given point in time and space.

8. Eighth Enochian Axiom: Subsets of Selfs are mutually exclusive.

9. Ninth Enochian Axiom: Subsets of Worlds may be either exclusive or inclusive.

10. Tenth Enochian Axiom: The essence of each Monad allows multitudinous expression, but no Self can ever separate itself from, or exist independently of, its World.

Although these axioms may at first appear confusing, a little study and thought will reveal their simplicity. They express an old poetic and mystical definition of humankind as a circle, whose center is nowhere and whose circumference is everywhere. If we think of the center as monadic consciousness (the Self) and the circumference as infinite

Space (the World of the Self), then it becomes obvious that the Enochian Monad Model is but a slight enhancement of this ancient mystical definition of humankind.

The Enochian Monad Model is thus a modern expression of an ancient idea. It does not, in itself, propose anything new. The ancient Egyptians, for example, symbolized the Self as a winged globe; the globe was a consciousness-center whose mobility was symbolized by the pair of wings. Egyptians considered centers to be masculine and circumferences to be feminine. Thus they personified the World in the goddess Nut (or Nuit), who is often shown arched over it. She represented the sky exoterically, and infinite Space esoterically. The winged globe was a symbol for the god Horns. This symbolism is repeated throughout western occultism, and is included in the Monad Model of Enochian Physics as well.

DEITIES AND HIERARCHIES

Enochian Magick denies the existence of a personal, absolute Deity, or God. Instead, the Enochian view of God agrees with the Buddhist teaching of a plurality of deities, with none supreme. The word *supreme* implies an end beyond which we cannot go; Enochian

Physics accepts no such limitations. Existence is infinite and unbounded. There are no limits to it, and therefore there can be no supreme being. However, there *are* intelligent rulers of each world, each planet, each sun, and so on. Enochian Magick establishes the rulers for each of the four Watchtowers as follows:

OROIBAHAOZPI–Air
MPHARSLGAIOL–Water
MORDIAIHKTGA–Earth
OIPTEAAPDOKE–Fire

These names are called the *Holy Names of God*, where "God" is the ruler of our universe (supreme in a relative sense only). In Enochian Magick, a god is only supreme with reference to a Universe or World. Other gods are supreme in other Worlds and Universes. This is a result of the Law of Hierarchies, which states that from the highest realms of spirit to the lowest levels of matter, everything in between is composed of a host of Gods, Monads or life-atoms, arranged in a myriad of hierarchies.

According to the Enochian Monad Model, every entity or "divine spark" enters the Cosmic Planes of Manifestation as an unselfconscious life-atom. Life-atoms slowly evolve into self-conscious Monads, and these slowly evolve into Gods as they undergo karmic evolution on the cosmic planes. Therefore the only real difference between a life-atom, a human being and a god is evolution in time. The monadic essence of each is identical. A life-atom can be defined as an immature God. A God can be defined as a highly-evolved life-atom. The chief of a hierarchy is called the Hierarch. We are the Hierarch of our body if we consider our body to be a hierarchy of cells and organs. Enochian Magick views each Watchtower as a hierarchy. The Hierarch of each Watchtower is called a King. The four Enochian Kings are BATAIVAH - Air; RAAGIOSL - Water; IKZHIKAL - Earth; and EDLPRNAA - Fire.

Each Watchtower is divided into six subhierarchies. The Hierarch of each of these is called a Senior. Each Watchtower is also divided into four subquadrants, whose Hierarchs are called Archangels. These are further divided up into smaller hierarchies, whose rulers are called Angels. In this way, the entire universe, visible and invisible, is teeming with beings in varying states of self-consciousness.

REINCARNATION

Reincarnation (rebirth) is caused by a desire for life. It is the creative urge for self-expression that maintains the cycle of reincarnation for us on the Cosmic Planes of Manifestation.

Figure 11. Stele of Revealing

Above the highest Aethyr, LIL, there is no time or space as we know it. Furthermore, there is no observable difference between one thing and any other thing. Above the great Ring-Pass-Not of LIL, we cannot say if countless hosts of identical beings exist, or if there is only one single Being. But immediately below this Ring-Pass-Not, we can begin to distinguish differences. Time and space make faint flickering promises of things to come. Life stirs into a state of expectation.

In the first expression of life, the monadic consciousness center sees itself as a Self and everything else as a World (that which is not a part of itself). With time, it seeks further definition of these two things. This has the effect of further separating the Self from its World. The Self is emphasized in the first Aethyr, LIL. When consciousness focuses on the World, it has already descended to the second Aethyr, ARN. The stage of defining the relationship between the two is in the third Aethyr, ZOM. Here the Self easily manipulates the World according to its True Will. In the eighth Aethyr, ZID, the Self takes on a special form known as the Holy Guardian Angel, the inner spiritual nature of man. Gradually, the Self descends into time and space until it reaches the tenth Aethyr, ZAX, known as the Great Outer Abyss.

When descending through the Abyss, the Self learns that forms are reality and that the formless is unreal because it is unsubstantial. As a result, the World of the Self polarizes into forms upon a formless background. The message of KHORONZON, the Archdemon of ZAX, is to desire the forms and to fear the formless.

The Self descends the Aethyrs learning the laws or ground rules of this universe as it goes. In TAN, for example, it gains a general sense of the ethics and morals of this world. It develops a rudimentary sense of right and wrong, and learns that all things in this universe cycle from one stage to another. In ASP, the Self forms the Reincarnating Ego as a result of its ability to define itself. While encountering others, it joins those who are karmically related to it. It joins a life-wave, a special group that makes general agreements and understandings easier. Such life-waves tend to express themselves in time and space together, and thus, incarnate together.

Eventually the Self, together with its life-wave, reaches the lowest of the Aethyrs. Here it waits for conditions to be karmically right on the physical plane for an incarnation. From this point on, the Self cycles between Earth and ASP. This periodic cycling is the reincarnation cycle. The details of each incarnation have a large degree of possible variation, depending on the individual Self. However, in general, each Self takes on a succession of lives on Earth, learning and growing as it goes. There is no "god" forcing the Self to reincarnate. Each entity does so on its own. It may undergo an incarnation in an attempt to right a past wrong (out of a sense of guilt) or it may feel like it has earned another life (out of a sense of deserving reward). It may simply do so out of a desire to express itself in flesh again. If evolved sufficiently, it may deliberately elect to incarnate so that it may help others less fortunate. Such a Self will often become a teacher, doctor, religious leader or humanitarian.

The idea that the body is like a suit of clothes that is put on at birth, and taken off at death, is naive. The human personality does not reincarnate, but dies on the astral plane in what is sometimes called the second death. When a person dies, the Self leaves the body of flesh and enters the subtle body, called the Body of Light. Someday that Self will send out another expression of itself into the lower planes and will reincarnate. According to Enochian Magick, the ego does not reincarnate. It is the individuality rather than the personality, the spirit rather than the soul, that reincarnates.

THE SIX FORCES OF MAGICK

Enochian Magick recognizes six primary forces in the manifested cosmic planes of existence as follows:

1. Divine Force. This is the Supreme Force relative to our universe. The forces of light and heat are but pale reflections of this highly penetrating force.

2. Mind Force. This is the power of the mind, and includes various stages, from the highest, wisdom and intuition, to the lowest, the logic and reason of the intellect. This power is symbolized by either the Sword or Dagger, which represents the mind's penetrating power. This force manifests chiefly as (a) Sensation; (b) Conceptualization; (c) Memory; and (d) Ego.

3. Will Force. When properly trained and disciplined, the force of will-power plays a major role in magickal operations. It is considered masculine in nature.

4. Thought Force. This force should not be confused with Mind Force. It often takes the form of projection, in order to produce external effects us (whereas Mind Force is chiefly internal). It is the occult force that continually projects fundamental subjective ideas of the Self outward into the World.

5. Creative Force. This is the Kundalini of eastern Tantrism. It manifests as electromagnetism. It is located in its unmanifested state in the subtle body at a point corresponding to the base of the spine in the physical body. When aroused, it rises upward into the psychic centers (or chakras) of the subtle body and activates them. It is considered feminine in nature.

6. Word Force. This is the power of letters, speech and music to influence things. It is the power of the mantra and japa of the East. The power of sound has long been known in the west. God is said to have created by uttering the Word. Similarly, every Magus must proclaim his or her own Word.

RESULTS OF THE ENOCHIAN MONAD MODEL

The Enochian Monad Model explains how Enochian Magick works and what it can and cannot do. By strengthening the will and controlling the mind (both of which have expressions of the Self), the magician can bring about changes in his or her environment and in others around him or her (the World). Everything one can possibly observe, anytime, anywhere, must first enter into one's World. There is no such thing as "only" a hallucination or "merely" an illusion. If a person perceives something, then that something is real—relative to him or her. Dreams are real—relative to the dreamer. Poverty and disease are some people's reality, while to others they are merely concepts. What one observes is largely controlled by one's karma, both individual and collective. A magician is a person who can consciously control his or her observations; to the extent that the magician is successful, he or she is said to have "eliminated his or her karma."

The ultimate goal of the Enochian magician is conscious control of his or her observations. By practicing Enochian Magick, one can establish this control to some degree on all the Cosmic Planes of Manifestation.

Dream control is a first step. Virtually all advanced magicians can consciously direct their dream contents according to their wills. Like a movie director, if the plot of a dream approaches something unpleasant or unwanted, the will can change it appropriately and the dream will continue (it is thus impossible for an advanced magician to have a nightmare). This ability is relatively easier to practice while dreaming than it is in the waking state. The reason is that with each Cosmic Plane leading toward matter, the collective karma (or the influences of the overlapping Worlds) increases in strength. The Self inherently has more control over the World on the astral plane than on the physical. On the mental plane control is even stronger. To compensate for this natural loss of ability, special techniques must be used to enhance the Self's control. This is the reason for breathing exercises and meditation rituals. With practice, the Self can be made to control its World on the physical plane to a remarkable extent (there *are* definite limits, however).

The main point to remember is that the Self controls, consciously or unconsciously, whatever enters into its World. In effect, it lets things in and then observes and reacts to them. For example, it can let an idea in which then later expresses itself physically. The idea "I am hungry" can eventually lead to the physical act of eating. Magickal control can also prevent unwanted things from entering the World.

The mental body is extremely busy interacting with other mental bodies. Normally one is not consciously aware of these continuous communications with other Selves. However, (whether we are conscious of it or not,) everyone uses mental telepathy all the time. We are literally bombarded by thoughts and emotions all the time. Every thought that goes through one's mind came from someone else and will go out into the mind of another (who may or may not become consciously aware of it). Simply entertaining a thought gives it strength. Thoughts feed on the psychic vitality of the mental body and grow according to how many people concentrate on them. The key to controlling one's World is thus tied to controlling this continuous flow of ideas, thoughts and emotions that swirl through one's subtle body. Yogic techniques are excellent tools for this task. The well-known power of positive thinking can also be useful to the magician. To a large extent, just realizing that one's World *can* be controlled by one's thoughts is a large step toward that goal.

In addition to *preventing* others from influencing him or herself, the magician can also *influence* others. Because of this, mature responsibility is needed and ethical development encouraged. By concentrating on a specific thought, the trained magician can successfully project that thought into the mental atmosphere of another Self, where it may then be accepted into that other's World as a reality. The World of another person can thus be influenced by the Self of the magician, to the extent that their Worlds interpenetrate. This is the familiar phenomenon of "spell casting" associated with stereotypical witches and Magick users. The effectiveness of such operations is directly proportional to the will of the magician and the ability of the recipient to control his or her own observations.

According to Enochian Magick, life in the higher planes will be similar to our life on Earth. When a person dies, for example, he or she will take his or her hopes, fears, successes and failures with him or her. If we desired something during this life, chances are we will continue to do so in the heavens of the lower Aethyrs, or wherever we gravitate. Our fears and guilts will similarly accompany us. There is no such things as oblivion or annihilation, any more so than there is such things as empty space. Karma *must* be worked out, now or later, here or somewhere else.

But as we will take our problems with us, we will also carry along our achievements. If we have learned control over our lives, then control over our after-death experiences, as well as our rebirth experiences, are equally assured. This means that spiritual development and progress can continue beyond the span of a single life on this planet. This is the great promise of Enochian Magick.

THE BODY OF LIGHT

The doctrine of the Body of Light is very old. It was well known, for example, in ancient

Egypt. It is a general term for the subtle body, which is actually composed of a divine body, a spiritual body, a causal body, a mental body, an astral body and an etheric body. The table below shows the main parts of humankind's Body of Light used in Enochian Magick, with Egyptian and modern Theosophical equivalents for comparison.

Parts of The Body of Light

Enochian	Egyptian	Theosophy
etheric	khaibit	linga-sarira
astral	ka	kama
mental	ba	lower manas
causal	sahu	upper manas
spiritual	khu	buddhi
divine	khabs	atma

TECHNIQUES

The two main techniques used in Enochian Magick are *skrying* and travel in the Body of Light, which is also called travel in the Spirit Vision. However, before these are to be used in a magickal operation, one must first draw a magic circle in which to work.

1. Consecrating a Circle. Enochian magicians always begin magickal operations by consecrating a circle. The circle is considered to be an ideal workspace for magickal operations. Many magicians like to draw or paint a circle

on the floor of their workroom. After drawing a circle, write the names of the elements in their appropriate directions as follows:

BITOM in the South	Fire, red
NANTA in the North	Earth, black
HKOMA in the West	Water, blue
EXARP in the East	Air, yellow

2. Skrying. Skrying is the practice of gazing into a crystal (Dee and Kelly used a crystal shewstone). The crystal is used as a tool to focus the mind on a desired goal. A light source is critical for this operation. The Sun, a lamp or a candle are the three main light sources normally used. The crystal must be between the light source and the eye. Let your eyes penetrate into the crystal while your mind concentrates on the goal of the operation. This method is also used to communicate with the deities who reside in the Watchtowers and Aethyrs.

3. Spirit Vision. Traveling in the Body of Light is the process of having the mind leave the physical body without the lapse of consciousness experienced during sleep. With the technique of traveling in the Spirit Vision, your mind will be able to leave your body with full consciousness and memory. This is the main technique used to visit the Watchtowers and Aethyrs; it's also one of the first tasks an Enochian magician must learn.

The term "Spirit Vision" implies perception above and beyond the physical (sometimes called astral traveling). Earth particles cannot leave the physical plane any more than Water particles can leave the astral plane, or Air particles can leave the mental. Consciousness, however, can travel throughout the manifested Cosmic Planes.

A physical body is limited to its space-time continuum, but consciousness has the ability to enter other continuums. In fact, it does this periodically in the states called sleep and death. The wave-like nature of consciousness allows it to radiate outwardly through the physical body in the waking state, to radiate outwardly through the astral body during the dream state, and to radiate outwardly through the mental body during the deep sleep state. The trained will can control the direction of consciousness and can focus it in all of the subplanes of the Cosmic Planes.

Consciousness is always positioned within a body or vehicle. So wherever consciousness may be, it will have a corresponding body suited to its environment. On the astral plane, for example, consciousness will be focused within an astral body having appropriate astral senses. The Watchtower Squares of the Watchtower of Water are visited in the astral body. The Squares of the Watchtower of Air are visited in the mental body, and so on.

WHAT ARE THE REAL DANGERS
OF ENOCHIAN MAGICK?

The dangers of Enochian Magick have at certain times been blown out of all proportion, and at other times carelessly denigrated. Aleister Crowley, for example, casually dismissed its dangers, and his writings leave the risks to the student's karma. On the other hand, several groups of the Golden Dawn refuse to practice Enochian Magick at all because they believe it is far too dangerous to meddle with. The truth lies in the middle of these two extremes. There are very real dangers associated with the practice of Enochian Magick. However, proper preparation can significantly reduce or eliminate these dangers. Is Enochian Magick completely safe to practice? No. Is it dangerous? Yes. Is it *too* dangerous? No; not if safeguards are used and one is properly prepared beforehand. It is like skydiving. Many people enjoy this sport every day without being harmed. But if a skydiver does not prepare himself or herself and the necessary equipment properly before a dive, the results can be devastating.

Probably the best-known danger is associated with the Enochian alphabet. A terrible potential is said to exist inherently in the letters of the Angelic alphabet, since you write out the name of a deity using the Angelic letters, and speak that name aloud but once, you could be visited by the deity in one form or another. Knowing the name of a deity (and this includes demons) establishes a psychomagnetic link between a magician and that deity. According to an ancient Egyptian text, "the life of a person is invested in his name." From the earliest days, humankind realized that the name of any living being had a subtle link with that being, and that by knowing a being's name you could control it to some degree. Likewise, the general rule is that to control an Enochian deity or demon, one must know its name. Once the name is known the awareness itself produces a subtle link with that deity. This link is sufficient, in some cases, to either allow one to go to the deity or to allow the deity to come to oneself. Because of this, special banishing rituals have been devised to allow the link to be severed, when necessary. Special invoking rituals have also been devised to re-establish the link, when desired.

As a simple example, consider the demon Hate. Once you become familiar with the idea of hatred, with which the name Hate is associated, you will be capable of hatred yourself. In a sense, your mental concentration on the name and its meaning opens a subtle attraction to the emotion itself, and you open yourself up to the demon of Hate, who could possess you at almost any time. The degree of susceptibility to establishing such links is karmic, and varies with individuals. Obviously, as far as Enochian deities are concerned, we will be more susceptible to this danger the more we believe in their reality. Most people refuse to believe they are real, and this belief protects them. In order to practice Enochian Magick, you must accept the reality of its deities. This acceptance will increase your susceptibility to their influences, as well as their danger to you. It is an unavoidable situation, but awareness is the first step in protection.

The real danger with Enochian Magick is not that a monster will jump out at you. The real danger is that the practice of Enochian magick—treading the path of the Great Work—will by its very nature precipitate much of your stored karma. Past karmic debts, known collectively as one's "karmic burden," can naturally be worked off over many future lifetimes. When the Great Work is attempted, one of the results is the dissipation of one's karmic burden. In effect, the karma that would normally take lifetimes to work out is worked out in this lifetime. Obviously this situation is not limited to Enochian Magick, but is true for all paths of the Great Work.

There are several safeguards a magician can use to reduce the dangers involved in the practice of Enochian Magick. The most obvious is to obtain knowledge. Know what you are doing and why you are doing it. Ignorant behavior, even when one's motives are pure, usually ends in disaster. Another is to cultivate a sincere love for your fellow human beings—a true desire to help others. Compassion is a necessity for work in the higher Aethyrs, and without it you will be in very great danger indeed. Morality aside, it turns out that strong feelings of compassion and selfless love coat the aura with a protective shield that few demons can penetrate. Without compassion, the ego will quite often have fear for itself in some form or another. It turns out that fear attracts demons of the worst sort, and can be ruinous for many magickal operations. The magician must conduct his or her exercises without fear. Perfect love casts out fear, and though it may sound trite in today's world, nevertheless it is true that love is the best and surest safeguard a magician can have.

WHAT IS ENOCHIAN YOGA?

The word *Yoga* means "to unite" or "to yoke together." The ultimate goal of Yoga is to unite the personal self with the spiritual Self, the human with the divine. The goal of Magick (or at least of High Magick) is also to unite the personal self with the spiritual Self (which Enochian Magick calls the Holy Guardian Angel). Thus the aims of Yoga and Magick are identical.

Probably the central difference between Magick and Yoga (especially Raja Yoga) is in their practice or application. Magick employs many devices designed to bring the physical body, speech and mind of the magician into play together. Raja Yoga prefers to downplay the physical body, and focuses mainly on mental techniques such as visualization. However, virtually all forms of Yoga teach breathing techniques which, to a degree, bring the physical body into play. Tantric Yoga often employs physical exercises and other means of using the body. However, Yoga almost never uses physical devices such as the weapons and talismans essential to the practice of Enochian Magick.

Enochian Yoga, however, allows us the option of using either physical or psychic devices. By using the Magickal Imagination, a psychic circle can be drawn, psychic weapons can be used for protection, and psychic talismans can be used for operations in the Body of Light. It is easier to effect Magickal results with physical devices, but not essential, so long as your Magickal Imagination is well developed. (You will notice that the term *operation* is used in connection with doing Magick. In Yoga, the yogi is said to conduct *yoga's* or *meditations*. In Magick, the magician is said to conduct *operations*.)

A yogi also typically enters into meditation without preliminary consecration of his area or banishment of unwanted influences, while a magician typically begins an operation by establishing a work area (usually in the form of a circle) and then consecrating it by banishing potential negative influences. A yogi typically ends his yoga without banishing influences from his work area; a magician will usually perform a final banishing ritual to sever any psychic links established during the operation. Those who practice Enochian Yoga should conduct in-depth consecrations and banishments as a psychic safety measure. With practice and experience, these exercises can be minimized.

One of the chief goals of Enochian Magick is to enter the Body of Light and travel into the Watchtowers and Aethyrs of the Magickal Universe. The goals of Enochian Yoga are identical; only the techniques are different. The Enochian yogi can enter the Aethyrs and Watchtowers with the same degree of skill and efficiency as an Enochian magician. The yogi can also meet the Enochian deities and converse with them.

WHAT IS ENOCHIAN TAROT?

Most people use the Tarot for divination. This was apparently the main use applied by the Gypsies. Another common use was for entertainment. In this form, the Tarot was used as a game, possibly a game of chance like modern poker and other card games. However, a deeper and more profound use was discovered by a few others. These were seekers after truth. They were people who struggled to learn about themselves and the world around them. For them, the Tarot was not a game but a mirror into which they could see themselves.

The highest use of the Tarot is as a system of enlightenment. It is a map into realms of spiritual bliss and a record of humankind's relationship with the cosmos. It is also a textbook of occult teachings. The Golden Dawn equates each Tarot trump card with a path on the Qabalistic Tree of Life. For this system, it is a symbolic map of inner space describing the highways of consciousness, from the loftiest spiritual heights of divinity down to the material world of human beings and matter. Seen in this light, the purposes of the Golden Dawn and Enochian Tarot are identical. Although the pathways are slightly different, they take one's consciousness over the same terrain and allow their users to reach the same states and stages of consciousness.

WHAT ARE THE PRIMARY RITUALS OF ENOCHIAN MAGICK?

The two main rituals in Enochian Magick are the Pentagram and the Hexagram Rituals below. These rituals are given as *examples only* and are not intended for use without proper preparation. Please study *Enochian Magic: A Practical Manual or An Advanced Guide to Enochian Magick* before using either of the rituals.

THE PENTAGRAM RITUAL

Step 1: Stand. Touch your forehead and say: "ZAH" (zod-ah).

Step 2: Touch your left breast and say: "ONDOH" (oh-doh).

Step 3: Touch your right shoulder and say: "MIH" (mee-heh).

Step 4: Touch your left shoulder and say: "BUZD" (boo-zod-deh).

Step 5: Touch both hands together on your right breast and: say: "Z "PAID" (pah-ee-deh).

Step 6: Turn to the East, trace a yellow Pentagram of Air before you and say: "Z "EXARP" (etz-ar-peh).

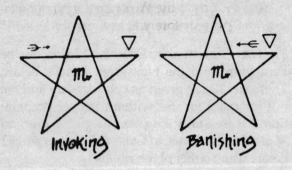

Figure 12. Pentagram of Air

Step 7: Turn to the South, trace a red Pentagram of Fire before you and say, "BITOM" (bee-toh-meh).

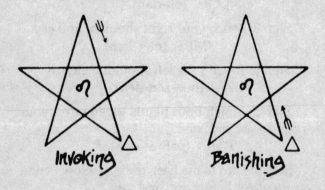

Figure 13. Pentagram of Fire

Step 8: Turn to the West, trace a blue Pentagram of Water before you and say, "HKOMA" (heh-koh-mah).

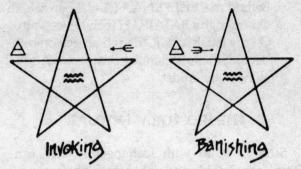

Figure 14. Pentagram of Water

Step 9: Turn to the North, trace a black Pentagram of Earth before you and say, "NANTA" (nah-en-tah).

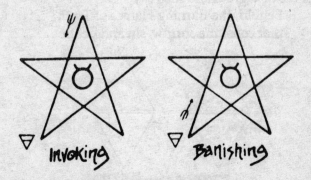

Figure 15. Pentagram of Earth

Step 10: Face the North, extend your arms outward to form a cross and say:
> Before me, IKZHIKAL (ee-keh-zeh-hee-kal).
> Behind me, EDLPRNAA (eh-del-par-nah-ah).
> On my right, BATAIVAH (bah-tah-ee-vah).
> On my left, RAAGIOSL (rah-ah-gee-oh-sel).
> Behold, the four flaming pentagram And I alone in the midst.

THE HEXAGRAM RITUAL

Step 1: Stand with feet together, left arm down at your side and right arm out before you.

Step 2: Turn to the East and say, "IVITDT" (ee-veh-ee-teh-deh-teh) while tracing the yellow Hexagram of Air before you. Say each letter of the formula while tracing a corresponding side of the hexagram and then say:
> Behold, the Burning Flames of Truth
> that consume sorrow, sin and death

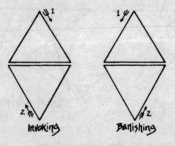

Figure 16. Hexagram of Ar

Step 3: Turn to the South and say, "ZTZTZT" (zod-teh-zod-teh-zod-teh) while tracing the red Hexagram of Fire before you. Say each letter of the formula while tracing a corresponding side of the hexagram, and then say:

> Behold, the Way of Love
> is to sacrifice All into the Cup.

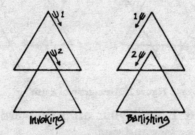

Figure 17. Hexagram of Fire

Step 4: Turn to the West and say, "IVITDT" (ee-veh-ee-teh-deh-teh) in the same manner as in Step 2, but trace the blue Hexagram of Water.

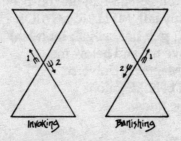

Figure 18. Hexagram of Water

Step 5: Turn to the North and say, "ZTZTZT" (zod-teh-zod-teh-zod-teh) in the same manner as in Step 3, but trace the black Hexagram of Earth.

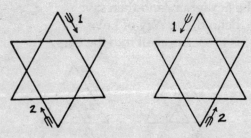

Figure 19. Hexagram of Earth

Step 6: Extend your arms outward in the form of a cross and say:

Before me, MORDIAIHKTGA
(moh-ar-dee-al-heh-keh-teh-gah).
Behind me, OIPTEAAPDOKE
(oh-ee-peh-teh-ah-ah-peh-doh-keh).
On my right, OROIBAHAOZPI
(oh-roh-ee-bah-hah-oh-zod-pee).
On my left, MPHARSLGAIOL
(meh-peh-har-sel-gah-ii-oh-leh).
Above me and below me,
My Magickal Universe,
And behold, I alone
In the midst.

On the following pages you will find listed, with their current prices, some of the books now available on related subjects. Your book dealer stocks most of these and will stock new titles in the Llewellyn series as they become available. We urge your patronage.

TO GET A FREE CATALOG

To obtain our full catalog, you are invited to write (see address below) for our bi-monthly news magazine/catalog, *Llewellyn's New Worlds of Mind and Spirit*. A sample copy is free, and will continue coming to you at no cost as long as you are an active mail customer. Or you may subscribe for just $10 in the USA and Canada ($20 overseas, first class mail). Many bookstores also have *New Worlds* available to their customers. Ask for it.

TO ORDER BOOKS AND TAPES

If your book store does not carry the titles described on the following pages, you may order them directly from Llewellyn by sending the full price in U.S. funds, plus postage and handling (see below).

Credit card orders: VISA, MasterCard, American Express are accepted. Call toll-free in the USA and Canada at 1-800-THE-MOON.

Postage and Handling: Include $4 postage and handling for orders $15 and under; $5 for orders *over* $15. There are no postage and handling charges for orders over $100. Postage and handling rates are subject to change. We ship UPS whenever possible within the continental United States; delivery is guaranteed. Please provide your street address as UPS does not deliver to P.O. boxes. Orders shipped to Alaska, Hawaii, Canada, Mexico and Puerto Rico will be sent via first class mail. Allow 4-6 weeks for delivery. **International orders:** Airmail – add retail price of each book and $5 for each non-book item; Surface mail – add $1 per item.

Minnesota residents please add 7% sales tax.

Llewellyn Worldwide
P.O. Box 64383 L-716, St. Paul, MN 55164-0383, U.S.A.

For customer service, call (612) 291-1970.

Prices subject to change without notice.

ANGEL MAGIC
The Ancient Art of Summoning & Communicating
with Angelic Beings
by Geoffrey James

One of the most universal religious beliefs is that a magician can harness the power of spiritual beings to gain influence and power over the physical world. The highest and most beautiful manifestation of this belief is Angel Magic, the art and science of communication with spiritual beings. Angel Magic is a set of ritual practices that is believed to control angels, daimons, fayries, genies, and other personifications of the elements, the planets, and the stars. Banned for centuries, it is at once the most practical and effective of the occult sciences.

This book traces Angel Magic from its birth in folk magic and shamanism through centuries of oppression to its greatest flowering in works of the great magi of the Renaissance. You will learn how this system of magic was almost lost until the researchers of magical lodges (such as the Order of the Golden Dawn) saved it from obscurity. What's more, you will witness accounts of the modern day practice of this curious and powerful art.

1-56178-368-9, 224 pgs., 6 x 9, illus., softcover $12.95

THE ENOCHIAN WORKBOOK
The Enochian Magickal System
Presented in 43 Easy Lessons
by Gerald J. and Betty Schueler

Enochian Magic is an extremely powerful and complex path to spiritual enlightenment. Here, at last, is the first book on the subject written specifically for the beginning student. Ideally suited for those who have tried other books on Enochia and found them to be too difficult, *The Enochian Workbook* presents the basic teachings of Enochian Magic in a clear, easy-to-use workbook.

The authors have employed the latest techniques in educational psychology to help students master the information in this book. The book is comprised of 11 sections, containing a total of 43 lessons, with test questions following each section so students can gauge their progress. You will learn how to conduct selected rituals, skry using a crystal, and use the Enochian Tarot as a focus for productive meditation. Also explore Enochian Chess, Enochian Physics (the laws and models behind how the magic works), and examine the dangers associated with Enochian Magic. Readers who complete the book will be ready to tackle the more complex concepts contained in the other books in the series.

One of the reasons why Enochian Magic is so hard to understand is that it has a special, complex vocabulary. To help beginning students, Enochian terms are explained in simple, everyday words, wherever possible.
0-87542-719-7, 360 pgs., 7 x 10, illus.,
16 color plates, softcover **$19.95**

THE ENOCHIAN MAGICK OF DR. JOHN DEE
The Most Powerful System of Magick in Its Original, Unexpurgated Form
Geoffrey James
(formerly *The Enochian Evocation of Dr. John Dee*)

Dr. John Dee's system of Enochian Magick is among the most powerful in the Western tradition, and it has been enormously influential in the practices of the Order of the Golden Dawn. Though long out-of-print, this book has become an occult classic because it holds all the secrets of Dee's private magical workbooks, just as Dee recorded them in the late 16th century.

This indispensable treasure of Enochian lore offers the only definitive version of the famous Angelical Calls or Keys, conjurations said to summon the angels of the heavenly sphere—as well as all the practical information necessary for the experienced magician to reproduce Dee's occult experiments, with details on how to generate the names of the angels, create Enochian talismans, and set up an Enochian temple. Here readers will find the only available version of Dee's system of planetary and elemental magic, plus other material sure to fascinate a new generation of students of Enochian Magick. Explore the source texts that inspired MacGregor Mathers, Aleister Crowley, Israel Regardie, and a host of others and learn to practice angelic magick!

1–56718–367–0, 6 x 9, 248 pp., illus. $14.95

THE ANGELS' MESSAGE TO HUMANITY
Ascension to Divine Union
Powerful Enochian Magick
Gerald and Betty Schueler

Initiate yourself into one of the most enriching and powerful systems of magic anywhere. *The Angels' Message to Humanity* presents a radical, new system of 88 graded paths based on mandalas created from the five Enochian tablets. Incorporating ritual magic, visualization, yoga, and mantras, nothing apart from this book is needed for these initiations.

The revised pathworking rituals in *The Angels' Message to Humanity* allow a magician to fully explore the Enochian system of magick, alone or with others. Explore alternative methods of skrying and ritually working with the Watchtowers. Build the Enochian Cube as a powerful, three-dimensional model of the magickal universe through advanced pathworking rituals.

Geared to the intermediate or advanced magical student, this book is divided into easy-to-read text and endnotes containing helpful references and technical information, as well as 121 illustrations and 8 color plates. Explore the world of modern Enochian magick today!

1-56718-605-X, 7 x 10, 352 pp., illus., softcover $24.95

THE ENOCHIAN TAROT DECK
Created by Gerald and Betty Schueler
Painted by Sallie Ann Glassman

The Enochian Tarot is a deck of cards which is primarily used to foretell the future. Forecasting the future, however, is only a superficial use of the massive powers of the Enochian Tarot. Here is a powerful tool which allows you to look deep inside your subconscious and "see" the direction your life is taking. The Enochian Tarot is an easy-to-use system of self-discovery which allows you to see your relationship to God and the universe.

The Tarot is your map of life. With it you can choose the road you want to wander. Instead of being an uninformed victim of your subconscious will, you can gather your inner strength and consciously change the path your life is to take. The Tarot is your key to self-determination, and with that key you can open any door.

The Enochian Tarot Deck consists of 86 cards which are divided into 2 main sections: a Major Arcana and a Minor Arcana. The Major Arcana is a set of 30 picture cards which are also called The Greater Arcana, Trumps, Atouts, or Triumphs. These cards are symbolic representations of various cosmic forces such as Doubt, Intuition, Glory, etc. The Minor Arcana contains 56 cards which represent the Four Enochian Watchtowers. The Minor Arcana is divided into 4 "suits" called Earth, Water, Air, and Fire.

0-87542-708-1, boxed set: 86 cards with booklet $12.95

TETRAGRAMMATON
The Secret to Evoking Angelic Powers
and the Key to the Apocalypse
by Donald Tyson

In Western magick, "Tetragrammaton" is the holiest name of God. It is composed of the four Hebrew letters IHVH and is the occult key that unlocks the meaning behind astrological symbolism, the tarot, the mysteries of the Old Testament and the Book of Revelation, the kabbalah, the Enochian magick of John Dee, and modern ritual magick. It is nothing less than the archetypal blueprint of creation, the basis for such fundamental forms as the DNA double helix and the binary language of modern computers. Its true structure is the great arcanum of occultism, which has never before been explicitly revealed but only hinted at in obscure religious and alchemical emblems. Now, for the first time, its true structure is laid bare in a clear and unambiguous manner, allowing this potent key to open astounding vistas of understanding.

Tetragrammaton is a book for kabbalists, ritual occultists and anyone fascinated by the magic of the Bible. Those seeking proof for the coming of the Apocalypse will be captivated by the justification for Revelation in the Keys.
1-56718-744-7, 320 pgs., 7 x 10, softcover $24.95

ENOCHIAN PHYSICS
The Structure of the Magical Universe
by Gerald J. Schueler

Gerald Schueler has taken the latest discoveries of modern physics and compared them to the laws of Enochian Physics. He shows how the magical universe is a natural extension of Einstein's space/time continuum. The only ingredient that Einstein left out was consciousness. When this factor is included, the magical universe is revealed. According to modern physics, matter is a form of energy. In *Enochian Physics* you will see that this same energy, the energy of modern physics, is the very substance, or "matter," of the magical universe.

The book incorporates magick and the latest concepts in the ever-changing field of theoretical physics. Quantum mechanics, black and white holes, alchemy and levitation, quarks and the Big Bang, the four elements and the four elementary forces are all brought together within a Grand Unified System of the magical universe. Included are such tantalizing scientific puzzles as the fluidity of time, the possibility of parallel universes, matter and antimatter, and the fate of the stars and galaxies. Those seeking a clear explanation of magical phenomena such as invisibility, astral travel and psychic healing will find it in the pages of *Enochian Physics*. Anyone practicing magick or interested in how magick works should read this book.

0–87542–712–X, 400 pgs., 5¼ x 8, illus., softcover $12.95

WESTERN MANDALAS OF TRANSFORMATION
Astrological & Qabalistic Talismans & Tattwas
by Soror A.L. • Illustrated by Lloyd Nygaard

More than any other book, *Western Mandalas of Transformation* reveals the uses of astrological and Qabalistic talismans for your spiritual use. Now you can learn the mysteries hidden in the ancient system of magical squares—some of which have never been published in the Western Magical Tradition! Geared toward both the beginner and experienced Qabalist, step-by-step instructions teach you the correspondences for creating your own mandala-talismans; how to acquire a magical Guardian Angel; correct guidelines for obtaining spiritual guides; the traditional Golden Dawn magic seals and the powerful Tattwa system. This complete guide contains special sections on the meaning of numbers, planetary attributes and many kinds of symbols. You get explanations of the secret techniques for awakening these images in your subconscious to energize your chakra system and personal aura. There is also a section on Gematria for the seasoned Qabalist, and a full chapter on Daath. Instruction in *Western Mandalas of Transformation* clears up mistakes and "blinds" in many other talismanic books of this century and is accompanied by more than 150 illustrations for your ease of learning.

1-56178-170-8, 272 pgs., 7 x 10, illus., color plates $19.95